FOOD LOVERS

C000050526

SMOOTHIES & JUICES

FOOD LOVERS

SMOOTHIES & JUICES

RECIPES SELECTED BY JONNIE LÉGER

Trans Atlantic Press

For best results when cooking the recipes in this book, buy fresh ingredients and follow the instructions carefully. Note that as a general rule vulnerable groups such as the very young, elderly people, pregnant women, convalescents and anyone suffering from an illness should avoid dishes that contain raw or lightly cooked eggs.

For all recipes, quantities are given in standard U.S. cups and imperial measures, followed by the metric equivalent. Follow one set or the other, but not a mixture of both because conversions may not be exact. Standard spoon and cup measurements are level and are based on the following:

1 tsp. = 5 ml, 1 tbsp. = 15 ml, 1 cup = 250 ml / 8 fl oz.

Note that Australian standard tablespoons are 20 ml, so Australian readers should use 3 tsp. in place of 1 tbsp. when measuring small quantities.

Although the recipes in this book are believed to be accurate and true at the time of going to press, neither the authors nor the publisher can accept any legal responsibility or liability for any errors or omissions that may be made nor for any inaccuracies nor for any harm or injury that may come about from following instructions or advice given in this book.

CONTENTS

RASPBERRY AND ACAI BERRY SMOOTHIE

Ingredients
Serves 2

1¼ cups / 300 ml acai berry juice

12 oz / 350 g frozen raspberries

1 cup / 250 g natural yogurt

2 tbsp runny honey

To garnish:

Some raspberries

1 tsp demerara sugar

Method
Prep and cook time: 10 min

1 Put the acai berry juice into a blender. Add the frozen raspberries, yogurt and honey.

2 Whiz together until blended and really smooth. Pour into 2 glasses.

3 Dip the ends of 6 raspberries into the smoothie, then dip these raspberry tips into the demerara sugar. Thread the raspberries onto wooden skewers or cocktail sticks to serve.

RASPBERRY AND PEACH DRINK

Ingredients

Serves 2

1 peach, coarsely chopped

½ cup / 100 g raspberries

2 tbsp honey

1 tbsp flaked (slivered) almonds

2 tsp lemon juice

¼ cup / 50 ml grape juice

6 ice cubes

Well chilled sparkling mineral water, as needed

Method

Prep and cook time: 5 min

1 Place the peach, raspberries, honey, almonds, lemon juice, grape juice and ice cubes in a blender and pulse to a smooth purée.

2 Divide between 2 glasses; add mineral water to fill.

VANILLA SMOOTHIE

Ingredients

Serves 2

½ cup / 75 g cubed honeydew melon

1 firm banana, cut into chunks

1 cup / 250 g plain yogurt

1 vanilla bean, slit lengthwise and seeds scraped out

8 ice cubes

⅓ – ½ cup / 100 ml whipping cream

1 tbsp lime juice, or to taste

2 tsp brown sugar

Method

Prep and cook time: 15 min

1 Place the melon, banana, yogurt and vanilla seeds into a blender and pulse until smooth.

2 Continue blending, gradually adding the cream and ice cubes, until very creamy. Add lime juice to taste.

3 Divide the smoothie between 2 glasses and sprinkle with brown sugar.

4 Using a cook's blowtorch, caramelize the sugar on the surface of the smoothies and serve at once.

MELON JUICE

Ingredients

Serves 2

½ small honeydew melon,
seeded and cut into chunks

1 tsp maple syrup

2 tbsp lime juice

8 ice cubes

1 cup / 250 ml sparkling
mineral water

Garnish:

Melon balls, threaded onto
wooden skewers

Fresh mint leaves

Method

Prep and cook time: 10 min

1 Place the melon, maple syrup, lime juice and
4 ice cubes in a blender and blend thoroughly.

2 Divide between 2 glasses and add the remaining
ice cubes. Add mineral water if desired.

3 Garnish with the melon ball skewers and
mint leaves.

CAPPUCCINO SMOOTHIE

Ingredients

Serves 2

1¼ cups / 300 ml strong espresso coffee

2 handfuls crushed ice

1¼ cups / 300 ml milk

2 tbsp maple syrup

2 tsp dark chocolate, finely grated

Method

Prep and cook time: 5 min plus 30 min cooling time

1 Pour the espresso coffee into a jug and cool.

2 Put a couple of handfuls of crushed ice into a blender and add the coffee, milk and maple syrup.

3 Whiz everything together until smooth.

4 Pour into 2 glasses and sprinkle over the finely grated chocolate to serve.

GINGER DRINK

Ingredients
Serves 2

4 inch / 10 cm piece fresh ginger root, coarsely grated (reserve juice)

2 tbsp brown sugar

1 large lemon

2 cups / 475 ml sparkling mineral water

Fresh mint sprigs, to garnish

Method
Prep and cook time: 10 min plus 10 min standing time

1 Put the ginger and its juice into a pitcher (jug) and sprinkle in the sugar.

2 Zest and juice the lemon, then add the zest to the pitcher and mash with a pestle or with the tip of a rolling pin. Squeeze the lemon and add the juice to the pitcher.

3 Pour in the sparkling water. Allow to stand for 10 minutes; taste and add a little more sugar, if necessary.

4 Strain the ginger drink through a sieve and divide between 2 glasses with lots of ice and some sprigs of mint.

CARROT AND PINEAPPLE JUICE

Ingredients

Serves 2

1 pineapple, trimmed and peeled.

2 carrots, trimmed

1 zucchini (courgette), trimmed

Method

Prep and cook time: 10 min

1 Quarter the pineapple and cut away the central woody core. Cut into long thin wedges.

2 Put a glass under the juicer spout and press half the pineapple, carrots and courgette (zucchini) through the juicer.

3 Remove the filled glass and place another glass under the juicer spout. Press the remaining pineapple, carrots and courgettes through the machine and serve.

COCONUT AND BERRY SMOOTHIE

Ingredients

Serves 2

$1/3$ cup / 50 g blueberries

$1/3$ cup / 50 g redcurrants

2 tbsp brown sugar

3 tbsp desiccated coconut, toasted in a dry pan and cooled

$1/3$ – $1/2$ cup / 100 ml coconut milk

Generous $3/4$ cup / 200 ml milk

Method

Prep and cook time: 10 min plus 30 mins chilling

1 Lay the blueberries and redcurrants in a shallow dish and place in the freezer for about 30 minutes.

2 Purée the berries, sugar, 2 tbsp of the desiccated coconut, coconut milk and milk in a blender.

3 Pour into two glasses and serve sprinkled with the remaining desiccated coconut.

ORANGE AND PEACH DRINK

Ingredients

Serves 2

4 peaches, quartered

4 oranges, peeled, quartered

Garnish

2 sprigs fresh mint

Fresh fruit

Method

Prep and cook time: 5 min

1 Remove the stones from the peaches.

2 Press the peaches and oranges through a juicer.

3 Garnish each glass with mint leaves and some fresh fruit.

MANGO AND PINEAPPLE SMOOTHIE

Ingredients

Serves 2

2 large, ripe mangos, peeled

Juice of 1 lime, zest peeled off in thin strips and reserved

A few ice cubes

1/3 – 1/2 cup / 100 ml pineapple juice

1–2 tbsp honey

Well-chilled still mineral water, if required

Garnish:

Fresh mint leaves

Reserved lime zest

Method

Prep and cook time: 10 min plus 30 min chilling time

1 Cut the flesh away from either side of the mango stone and chop the flesh.

2 Lay the chopped mango in a shallow dish and place in the freezer for about 30 minutes.

3 Whiz the mango, lime juice, ice cubes, pineapple juice and honey in a blender. Well-chilled water can be added if necessary.

4 Divide the smoothie between 2 glasses and garnish with the strips of lime zest and mint leaves.

TROPICAL FRUIT SMOOTHIE

Ingredients

Serves 2

1 mango

2 bananas, sliced

1 cup / 250 g natural yogurt

6 tbsp crushed ice

1 passion fruit, halved

Method

Prep and cook time: 10 min

1 Score the mango flesh into slices and cut away from the skin. Reserve a couple of slices of mango to garnish.

2 Put the rest of the mango into a blender with the banana and natural yogurt. Whiz together until smooth.

3 Add the crushed ice and blend together again. Pour into 2 glasses.

4 Scoop out the seeds and juice from the passion fruit and spoon on top of the smoothies with the reserved mango slices.

HOT LEMON AND HONEY WITH CLOVES

Ingredients

Serves 2

3 lemons, halved

1¼ cups / 300 ml boiling water

4 tsp honey

1 tsp whole cloves (optional)

Method

Prep and cook time: 10 min

1 Squeeze the juice from 5 of the lemon halves and pour into a heatproof pitcher (jug) with the boiling water, stirring well.

2 Put 2 tsp honey into each of 2 warmed glasses and add the hot lemonade to fill.

3 Cut the remaining lemon half into wedges, stud with cloves (note—they have a strong flavor!) and place in the glasses.

KIWI FRUIT, MELON AND PEAR SMOOTHIE

Ingredients

Serves 2

2 kiwi fruit, peeled and chopped

¾ cup / 150 g chopped honeydew melon

1 small very ripe pear, peeled, cored and chopped

2 tbsp lemon juice

6 ice cubes

Confectioners' (icing) sugar to taste

Method

Prep and cook time: 15 min

1 Place the kiwi fruit, melon and pear into a blender with the lemon juice and ice; pulse until smooth.

2 Add confectioners' (icing) sugar to taste and serve.

CHILI MANGO COCKTAIL

Ingredients

Serves 2

1 red chili, sliced and deseeded

2 tbs lime juice

4 tsp agave syrup

1/3 – 1/2 cup / 100 ml elderflower cordial (made up from 2–3 tbsp of undiluted cordial plus cold water)

2 cups / 450 ml mango juice

4 handfuls ice cubes

4 tbsp grenadine

To garnish:

2 red chilies

2 sticks mango flesh, cut from a fresh fruit

Method

Prep and cook time: 15 min

1 Put the chili slices into a cocktail shaker and mash (muddle) with a long spoon.

2 Add the lime juice, agave syrup, elderflower cordial, mango juice and 2 handfuls of ice.

3 Pour the grenadine into the bottom of 2 tall glasses and add the rest of the ice.

4 Shake the cocktail shaker well and strain the juice into the glasses.

5 Garnish each glass with a chili and a stick of mango.

PEACH AND PASSION FRUIT SMOOTHIE

Ingredients
Serves 2

1 lb / 450 g can peaches in natural juice

1 banana, sliced

$^2/_3$ cup / 150 ml passion fruit juice

$^2/_3$ cup / 150 ml lowfat milk

1 passion fruit, halved, to garnish

Method
Prep and cook time: 5 min

1 In a blender or food processor, combine the canned peaches and their juice, banana, passion fruit juice and milk. Pulse until completely smooth and pour into 2 glasses.

2 Scoop out the passion fruit seeds and spoon them on top of each smoothie to garnish.

COCONUT AND BANANA SHAKE

Ingredients
Serves 2

1 ripe banana, chopped

$^1/_3$ – $^1/_2$ cup / 100 ml orange juice

$^1/_3$ – $^1/_2$ cup / 100 ml coconut milk, chilled

$^1/_3$ – $^1/_2$ cup / 100 ml buttermilk, chilled

1 tbsp brown sugar

Coconut flakes, to garnish

Method
Prep and cook time: 5 min

1 Put the banana, orange juice, coconut milk, buttermilk and brown sugar into a blender and pulse until smooth.

2 Pour into 2 glasses and serve garnished with coconut flakes

FROZEN STRAWBERRY DRINK

Ingredients

Serves 2

1 pint / 250 g strawberries, hulled

$^1/_3$ – ½ cup / 100 ml apple juice

2 tsp superfine (caster) sugar

2 tbsp lime juice

8 tbsp crushed ice

Garnish:

Fresh lemon balm leaves

Reserved strawberry

Method

Prep and cook time: 20 min plus 30 min chilling time

1 Lay the strawberries out in a single layer on a tray and place in the freezer for 30 minutes to freeze slightly. Reserve a strawberry for the garnish.

2 Place the strawberries, apple juice, sugar, lime juice and ice in a blender and pulse to a coarse purée.

3 Pour into glasses to serve and garnish with lemon balm and the reserved strawberry.

BLACKBERRY AND APPLE SMOOTHIE

Ingredients

Serves 2

1¼ cups / 250 g frozen blackberries, plus extra to garnish

2 tbsp honey

1 cup / 250 g forest fruits or blueberry yogurt

1¼ cups / 300 ml pressed apple juice

Method

Prep and cook time: 5 min

1 Put the frozen blackberries into a blender with the honey, yogurt and apple juice. Pulse until smooth and pour into 2 glasses.

2 Thread some blackberries onto 2 bamboo skewers or cocktail sticks and garnish the smoothies.

LEMON GRASS LEMONADE

Ingredients

Serves 2

1 stem lemon grass

Zest and juice of 2 large lemons

¼ cup / 50 g superfine (caster) sugar

2½ cups / 600 ml boiling water

10 ice cubes

Garnish:

2 stems lemon grass

2 mint sprigs

Method

Prep and cook time: 15 min plus 8 hours chilling

1 Trim off the base and top of the lemon grass stem; finely slice the remainder. Put the sliced lemon grass into a heatproof bottle or container and add the lemon juice, zest and sugar.

2 Pour over the boiling water. Cover and let steep overnight.

3 Stir and taste for sweetness, adding more sugar if needed. Strain the lemonade into 2 glasses.

4 Add ice cubes to fill and garnish with a lemon grass stem and mint sprig in each glass.

ICED FRUIT COCKTAIL

Ingredients

Serves 2

1 cup / 200 g mixed fruit (try grapefruit, apple, black grapes) cut into bite-size pieces

1 cup / 250 ml apple juice

2 tbsp lime juice

6 ice cubes

About 1 cup / 200 ml well-chilled sparkling mineral water

Method

Prep and cook time: 10 min

1 Thread the prepared fruit onto wooden skewers.

2 Pour the apple juice and lime juice into a blender. Add the ice cubes and pulse briefly.

3 Divide the juice between two glasses and add the fruit skewers. Add mineral water to fill.

PEAR AND ORANGE CRUSH

Ingredients

Serves 2

4 pears, peeled, cored and quartered

2½ cups / 600 ml cold water

Juice of 4 oranges

1 tbsp honey

Method

Prep and cook time: 20 min plus 1 hour cooling

1 Put the pears into a pan and cover with the water. Bring to a boil; reduce the heat and simmer for 5 minutes to soften the fruit.

2 Turn off the heat and let stand for 10 minutes.

3 Pour the pears and juice into a blender and pulse until completely smooth.

4 Pour the pear juice through a sieve into a pitcher. Add the orange juice and honey and transfer to a bottle. Refrigerate for 1 hour. Shake before serving.

ORANGE AND SEA BUCKTHORN DRINK

Ingredients

Serves 2

2/3 cup / 150 ml sweetened sea buckthorn purée*

½ cup / 125 ml freshly squeezed orange juice

2 cups / 500 ml buttermilk

Garnish:

1 sponge finger (ladyfinger biscuit), broken into small pieces

Orange zest

Fresh mint sprigs

Method

Prep and cook time: 5 min

1 Pulse the buckthorn purée, orange juice and buttermilk together in a blender until smooth. Pour into 2 glasses.

2 Serve garnished with the sponge finger, orange zest and mint.

*Sea buckthorn purée, made from the vitamin C-rich fruit of the sea buckthorn plant, can be found in natural food stores.

BEET AND CELERY DRINK

Ingredients

Serves 2

4 stalks celery

2 beets (beetroot) peeled and finely chopped (reserve 4 slices for garnish)

1/3–1/2 cup / 100 ml apple juice

Zest and juice of 1 lemon

1 sprig fresh lemon balm leaves, sliced into fine strips

2 tsp freshly grated ginger root

Garnish:

Reserved beet slices

Method

Prep and cook time: 15 min

1 Put on rubber gloves (to prevent beet stains) and push the celery and beets (beetroot) down the feeder tube of a juicer.

2 Pour into a pitcher and mix in the apple juice, lemon zest and juice, lemon balm strips and the ginger. Pour into two glasses.

3 Thread the reserved beet slices onto toothpicks (cocktail sticks) and serve with the drink as a garnish.

STRAWBERRY AND ALMOND SMOOTHIE

Ingredients

Serves 2

1 cup / 200 g ripe strawberries, hulled (reserve a few, sliced, for garnish)

2 tbsp ground almonds

2 tbsp elderflower liqueur

1¼ cups / 300 g cold plain yogurt

Garnish:

Flaked almonds

Strawberry slices

Method

Prep and cook time: 15 min plus 30 min chilling time

1 Place the strawberries in a shallow dish and freeze for 30 minutes until partially frozen.

2 Place the strawberries, ground almonds, liqueur and the yogurt in a blender and pulse until creamy.

3 Divide between 2 glasses and garnish with flaked almonds and strawberry slices.

BERRY AND BRAN DRINK

Ingredients

Serves 2

²/₃ cup / 100 g mixed berries (e. g. strawberries, blackberries; blueberries)

Juice of 2 oranges

2 tbsp lemon juice

¹/₃ – ½ cup / 100 ml carrot juice

1 tbsp oat bran

1 tbsp honey

Garnish:

6 blackberries threaded onto wooden skewers

Method

Prep and cook time: 10 min

1 Put the berries, orange juice, lemon juice and carrot juice into a blender and pulse to combine thoroughly.

2 Add the oat bran and honey and blend until smooth. Pour the drink into two small glasses and serve garnished with the blackberry skewers.

RASPBERRY, GRAPEFRUIT AND BANANA SMOOTHIE

Ingredients

Serves 2

3 bananas, sliced

¾ cup / 200 g frozen raspberries

1 tbsp honey

1¼ cups / 300 ml pink grapefruit juice

Garnish:

Fresh raspberries

Method

Prep and cook time: 5 min

1 Put the bananas, frozen raspberries, honey and grapefruit juice into a blender and pulse until the fruits are blended and smooth.

2 Pour into 2 glasses and serve topped with the raspberries.

APRICOT AND GINGER DRINK

Ingredients

Serves 2

1 inch / 2 cm piece fresh ginger root, peeled

2½ cups / 600 ml water

7 oz / 200 g dried apricots

2 tbsp caster (superfine) sugar

Method

Prep and cook time: 30 min plus chilling time

1 Chop the ginger and place in a saucepan with the water, the apricots and sugar. Bring to a boil, reduce the heat and simmer, covered, for 20 minutes until the apricots are tender.

2 Transfer to a blender and pulse until smooth. Strain into a pitcher and chill thoroughly.

AVOCADO AND CUCUMBER DRINK

Ingredients

Serves 2

1 cucumber, chopped

1 ripe avocado, peeled and chopped

1 tbsp lime juice

1 scallion (spring onion), chopped

2 tsp chopped cilantro (coriander) leaves

Dash chili sauce

2½ cups / 600 ml cold water

Method

Prep and cook time: 15 min

1 Put the cucumber, avocado, lime juice, scallion (spring onion), cilantro (coriander) and chili sauce in a blender.

2 Add the cold water and pulse until smooth. Pour into 2 glasses and serve.

CARROT AND MANGO JUICE

Ingredients

Serves 2

2 large carrots, peeled

1¼ cups / 300 ml cold water

1 mango, peeled and chopped

²/₃ cup / 150 ml orange juice

Garnish:

1 celery stick, quartered

4 walnut halves

Method

Prep and cook time: 10 min plus 20 min standing time

1 Grate the carrots and put into a bowl with the cold water. Cover and leave for 20 minutes.

2 Put the mango into a blender with the orange juice. Pulse until smooth.

3 Hold a sieve over the blender and strain the carrot juice into it, discarding the shredded carrots. Pulse again to combine.

4 Pour into 2 glasses and garnish each with celery stalks and a couple of walnut halves.

PEAR YOGURT SHAKE WITH CINNAMON

Ingredients
Serves 2

1 medium-sized ripe pear, peeled, quartered, cored and chopped

Scant cup / 200 ml plain yogurt

2/3 cup / 150 ml whipping cream

1 tbsp acacia honey

½ tsp ground cinnamon

1 pinch nutmeg

Cinnamon sugar, to garnish

Method
Prep and cook time: 10 min

1 Put the pear, yogurt, cream, honey, cinnamon and nutmeg in a blender and pulse until smooth. For best results, the pear should be soft but not mushy. Yogurt and cream should be well chilled.

2 Pour into 2 glasses and sprinkle with cinnamon sugar to serve.

TOMATO GAZPACHO SMOOTHIE

Ingredients
Serves 2

14-oz / 400 g can diced tomatoes in juice

½ red bell pepper, seeded

½ cucumber, chopped

1 tbsp balsamic vinegar

1 tbsp cilantro (coriander leaves)

1 scallion (spring onion), chopped

1 garlic clove, peeled

Dash chili sauce

Crushed ice, as needed

Garnish:

2 watercress sprigs

Method
Prep and cook time: 20 min

1 In a blender, combine the tomatoes, bell pepper, cucumber, balsamic vinegar, cilantro (coriander leaves), scallion (spring onion), garlic and chili sauce.

2 Add a couple of handfuls of crushed ice and pulse until smooth.

3 Pour into 2 glasses and garnish each one with a watercress sprig.

VANILLA AND COCONUT SMOOTHIE

Ingredients

Serves 2

14 oz / 400 g can low-fat coconut milk

Crushed ice, as needed

1¼ cups / 300 g vanilla yogurt

1 banana, chopped

1¼ cups / 300 ml apple juice

Method

Prep and cook time: 5 min

1 Put the coconut milk, yogurt, banana and apple juice in a blender. Add the crushed ice as needed and pulse until smooth.

2 Pour into 2 glasses and serve.

PAPAYA AND APPLE DRINK

Ingredients

Serves 2

1 ripe papaya, peeled

2 tsp lime juice

1 tbsp honey

2 cups / 500 ml apple juice

Ice cubes, as needed

Garnish:

Lemon slices

Method

Prep and cook time: 10 min

1 Halve the papaya, scoop out the seeds and discard. Coarsely chop the fruit.

2 Put the papaya, lime juice, honey and apple juice into a blender and pulse until smooth.

3 Put several ice cubes into 2 glasses and pour in the papaya-apple drink. Garnish each glass with a slice of lemon.

CHERRY AND CRANBERRY SMOOTHIE

Ingredients

Serves 2

1 cup / 250 g frozen pitted dark sweet cherries

1¼ cups / 300 ml sweetened cranberry juice

1¼ cups / 300 g low-fat cherry yogurt

Method

Prep and cook time: 5 min

1 Put the frozen cherries, cranberry juice and yogurt into a blender and pulse into smooth.

2 Pour into 2 glasses to serve.

GRAPE JUICE MILKSHAKE

Ingredients

Serves 2

2 scoops vanilla ice cream

1¼ cups / 300 ml grape juice

1¼ cups / 300 ml milk

Garnish:

2 tsp honey

2 small bunches red grapes

1 tbsp caster (superfine) sugar

Method

Prep and cook time: 10 min

1 Put the vanilla ice cream into a blender with the grape juice and milk. Pulse to combine and pour into 2 glasses.

2 In a small shallow microwave-safe bowl, microwave the honey on High for 5 seconds to make it more liquid.

3 Dip the grapes into the honey, using a brush to help coat the grapes. Dip the grapes into the sugar, sprinkling over areas that aren't covered. Serve on the edge of the glasses, to garnish.

PAPAYA LASSI

Ingredients
Serves 2

1 ripe papaya, peeled, halved, seeded and chopped (reserve some for garnish)

2 tbsp lemon juice

1 tbsp honey

1 pinch vanilla bean seeds

1 cup / 200 g plain yogurt

$1/3 - 1/2$ cup / 100 ml milk

Garnish:

Reserved papaya segments

Method
Prep and cook time: 10 min

1 Put the papaya, lemon juice, honey, vanilla seeds, yogurt and milk into a blender; pulse until smooth and creamy.

2 Pour into glasses and serve garnished with papaya segments.

PINEAPPLE SMOOTHIE

Ingredients

Serves 2

1 small banana, peeled and sliced

$^2/_3$ cup / 100 g finely chopped fresh pineapple (reserve a few segments for garnish)

$^1/_3$–$^1/_2$ cup / 100 g plain yogurt

$^1/_3$–$^1/_2$ cup / 100 ml milk

1 tbsp lemon juice

1 pinch grated lemon zest

1–2 tbsp brown sugar

Garnish:

Pineapple segments

Method

Prep and cook time: 10 min

1 Place the banana and pineapple in a blender with the yogurt, milk, lemon juice, lemon zest and sugar. Blend thoroughly on the highest setting until smooth.

2 Pour into glasses and serve, garnished with the pineapple segments. Serve immediately as enzymes contained in fresh pineapple will eventually turn the drink bitter. This will not happen if canned pineapple is used.

BERRY AND POMEGRANATE LASSI

Ingredients
Serves 2

½ cup / 100 g frozen raspberries

½ cup / 100 g frozen blackcurrants

¼ cup / 50 g strawberries, hulled

1¼ cups / 300 g low-fat plain yogurt

1¼ cups / 300 ml pomegranate juice

Garnish:

2 tbsp chopped fresh mint leaves

Method
Prep and cook time: 10 min

1 Put the frozen raspberries, blackcurrants and strawberries, yogurt and pomegranate juice into a blender. Pulse until smooth.

2 Pour into 2 glasses and sprinkle over the chopped mint to garnish.

PINEAPPLE AND FENNEL COCKTAIL

Ingredients

Serves 2

1 pineapple, peeled, cored and chopped (reserve 2 small slices for garnish)

1 fennel bulb, trimmed and coarsely chopped – leaves reserved

6 ice cubes

Garnish:

Reserved pineapple slices

Reserved fennel leaves

Method

Prep and cook time: 15 min

1 Press both the fennel and pineapple through the feeder tube of a juicer.

2 Blend the juice and ice cubes in a blender until frothy. Divide between two glasses.

3 Serve garnished with the pineapple slices and fennel leaves.

BANOFFEE TOFFEE MILKSHAKE

Ingredients

Serves 2

2 bananas, sliced

2 cups / 500 ml milk

4 tbsp dulce de leche caramel*

2 scoops caramel ice cream

Garnish:

2 pecans, chopped

Method

Prep and cook time: 5 min

1 Put the bananas into a blender and add the milk, caramel and ice cream. Pulse until smooth.

2 Pour into 2 glasses and sprinkle over the pecans to garnish.

*Dulce de leche, an intensely sweet milk caramel made by boiling down sweetened milk, can be found in gourmet stores.

BELL PEPPER AND PAPAYA JUICE

Ingredients

Serves 2

4 red bell peppers, halved and seeded

2 papayas, peeled, seeded and coarsely chopped

Juice of 1 lime

Garnish:

Celery stalks

Method

Prep and cook time: 15 min

1 Push the bell peppers and papayas down the feeder tube of a juicer into 2 glasses.

2 Add the juice of half a lime to each glass; stir and serve garnished with a celery stalk.

LIME MARGARITA SMOOTHIE

Ingredients
Serves 2

2 large limes

2 tsp sea salt

¼ cup / 50 ml pressed apple juice

⅔ cup / 150 ml white grape juice

Crushed ice, as needed

Garnish:

Reserved finely grated lime zest

Method
Prep and cook time: 10 min

1 Finely grate the zest from the limes; reserve half for garnish and put the rest into a blender.

2 Juice the limes. Pour 1 tbsp of lime juice into a saucer and the sea salt in another.

3 Dip the rim of an upturned margarita glass into the lime juice, then the salt. Repeat with another glass.

4 Put the remaining lime juice into the blender with the apple juice, grape juice and ice. Blend until slushy.

5 Pour into the salt-rimmed glasses and sprinkle with reserved lime zest; serve immediately.

WATERMELON, STRAWBERRY AND LYCHEE SMOOTHIE

Ingredients

Serves 2

8 oz / 250 g watermelon, seeded and cut into chunks

5 oz / 125 g strawberries, hulled

1 banana, sliced

²/₃ cup / 150 g natural yogurt

²/₃ cup / 150 ml lychee juice

4 tbsp crushed ice

Garnish:

2 sprigs mint

Method

Prep and cook time: 15 min

1 Put the watermelon, strawberries, banana, yogurt, lychee juice and ice into a blender and pulse to combine.

2 Pour into 2 glasses and garnish each with a sprig of mint.

HEALTHY EGG AND WHEAT GERM SMOOTHIE

Ingredients

Serves 2

2 very fresh eggs, separated

2 tbsp acacia honey

1²/₃ cups / 400 ml whole milk

2 tbsp wheat germ

Freshly grated nutmeg

Ground cinnamon

Method

Prep and cook time: 20 min

1 With an electric mixer, beat the egg yolks and honey in a bowl until pale and frothy; set aside.

2 In a small saucepan, heat the milk, stirring, over medium-high heat until bubbles form at the edge of the pan (do not allow the milk to boil). Set aside to cool slightly.

3 In another bowl with a whisk or an electric mixer, beat the egg whites until stiff.

4 Add the warm milk and wheat germ to the egg yolk mixture and combine with an immersion (hand-held) blender until smooth and homogeneous.

5 Add nutmeg and cinnamon to taste, then fold in the stiff egg whites. Divide between 2 glasses and serve immediately.

WARM APPLE PUNCH

Ingredients

Serves 2

2 cups / 500 ml apple juice

1 cinnamon stick

4 juniper berries

Zest and juice of 1 orange

Garnish:

Red apple peel

2 cinnamon sticks

Method

Prep and cook time: 30 min

1 Put the apple juice, cinnamon stick and juniper berries into a large saucepan.

2 Add the orange juice and zest to the saucepan; bring to a boil, reduce the heat and simmer for 20 minutes to infuse the spices.

3 Strain the punch and ladle into 2 heatproof glasses. Garnish each with a cinnamon stick and a swirl of apple peel.

Published by Transatlantic Press

First published in 2011

Transatlantic Press
38 Copthorne Road, Croxley Green, Hertfordshire WD3 4AQ

© Transatlantic Press

Images and Recipes by StockFood © The Food Image Agency

Recipes selected by Jonnie Léger, StockFood

All rights reserved.

No part of this publication may be reproduced or transmitted in any form or by any means,
electronic or mechanical, including photocopying, recording,or any information storage and retrieval system,
without permission in writing from the copyright holders.

A catalogue record for this book is available from the British Library.

ISBN 978-1-907176-49-4

Printed in China